The Great Songs

Rolling Stones.

Wise Publications
London/New York/Sydney

Exclusive Distributors
Music Sales Limited,
8/9 Frith Street, London W1V 5TZ, England.
Music Sales Pty, Limited,
120 Rothschild Avenue, Rosebery, NSW 2018, Australia.

This book © Copyright 1984 by
Wise Publications
ISBN 0.7119.0593.2
Order No. AM 38225

Compiled by Peter Evans
Designed by Pearce Marchbank and Philip Levene
Cover Photograph by L.F.I.

Music Sales complete catalogue lists thousands of
titles and is free from your local music shop,
or direct from Music Sales Limited.
Please send a cheque/postal order for £1.50 for postage to
Music Sales Limited, Newmarket Road, Bury St Edmunds,
Suffolk IP33 3YB.

Printed in England by
J.B. Offset Printers (Marks Tey) Limited, Marks Tey.

The Great Songs of The Rolling Stones.

(This Could Be) The Last Time

Words & Music: Mick Jagger and Keith Richard

Out Of Time

Words & Music: Mick Jagger and Keith Richard

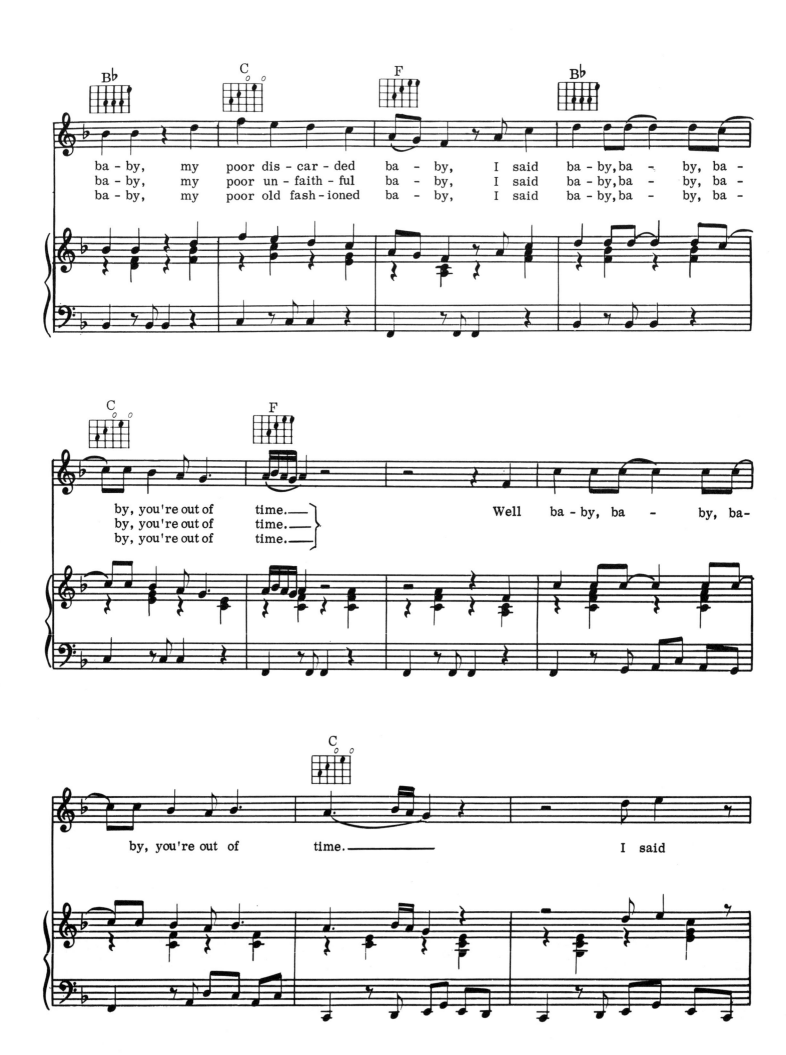

ba - by, ba - by, ba - by, you're out of   time._____

Yes, you are left   out;   out of there with -

out a doubt,___ 'cause ba - by, ba - by, ba - by, you're out of

time.   time.

It's All Over Now

Words & Music: B. and S. Womack

wor-ried she could ease my ach-ing head. But now she's here and there with

ev-'ry man in town, in-stead of trying to take me for that same old— clown

D7   C

opt. (8va)

— Be-cause I used to love her, but it's all o - ver

G

now.

1. 2. opt. 8va.   3.

Be-cause I

Lady Jane

Words & Music: Mick Jagger and Keith Richard

My sweet la - dy Jane, _____ when I see you a -
My dear la - dy Anne, _____ I've done what I
Oh, my sweet Mar - ie, _____ I wait at your

gain _____ your ser - vant am I; _____
can. _____ I must take my leave; _____
cue. _____ The sands have run out; _____

and will hum - bly re - main. ____
for prom - ised I am. ____
for your la - dy and me. ____

Just be dis -
The play is
When love is

pleased, my love.
run, my love.
nigh, my love.

On bend - ed knee my love.
Your time has come my love.
Her sta - tion's right my love.

I pledge my - self to la - dy Jane.
I pledge my soul to la - dy Jane.
Life is se - cure with la - dy Jane.

15

Have You Seen Your Mother, Baby

Words & Music: Mick Jagger and Keith Richard

I'm all a - lone, won't you give
The brave old world or the slide

all your sym - pa - thy to
to the depths of de -

mine?
cline.

al Coda

Tell ___ me a sto - ry ___ a - bout how ___ you a - dore me, ___ how we
Live ___ in the sha - dow, ___ how we see ___ through the sha - dow, ___ how we
Glimpse ___ through the sha - dow, ___ how we tear ___ at the sha - dow, ___ how we
Hate ___ in the sha - dow, ___ how we live ___ in your

sha - dow - y life. ___

Let It Bleed

Words & Music: Mick Jagger and Keith Richard

Well, we all ___ need some-one we can lean ___ on ___ And if you
___ need some-one we can bleed ___ on ___ And if you

want it, ___ Well, you can lean on me. ___ Yeah, we all
want to, ___ Well, you can bleed on me. ___ Yeah, we all ___

___ need some-one we can lean ___ on, ___ If you
___ need some-one we can bleed ___ on, ___ If you

need   some - one   we can dream __ on _____   and if you

want it, ___   Well, you can dream on   me. _____   Yeah, we all __

need   some - one   we can cream __ on, _____   if you

want to, ___   Well, you can cream on   me. _____   I was

dream-ing   of   a   steel __ gui - tar   en - gage - ment _____   when you

drunk my health— in scent-ed jas - mine tea._____ Yeah, you knifed—

— me in my filth - y, dirt-y base - ment— with that

jad-ed, fad-ed, jurk-y nurse. Oh,—what pleas-ant com-pa-ny! We all need—

— some-one we can feed— on,_____ and if you

want to,— Well, you can feed on me._____

Brown Sugar

Words & Music: Mick Jagger and Keith Richard

Gold — Coast slave — ship bound for
Beat - ing, — cold Eng-lish
I bet your ma - ma was a

cot - ton fields, — sold — in a mar-ket down in New Or - leans. — Scarred
blood runs hot, — la — dy of the house won-d'rin where it's gon-na stop. House
Tent Show queen, — and — all her girl friends were sweet six - teen. — I'm

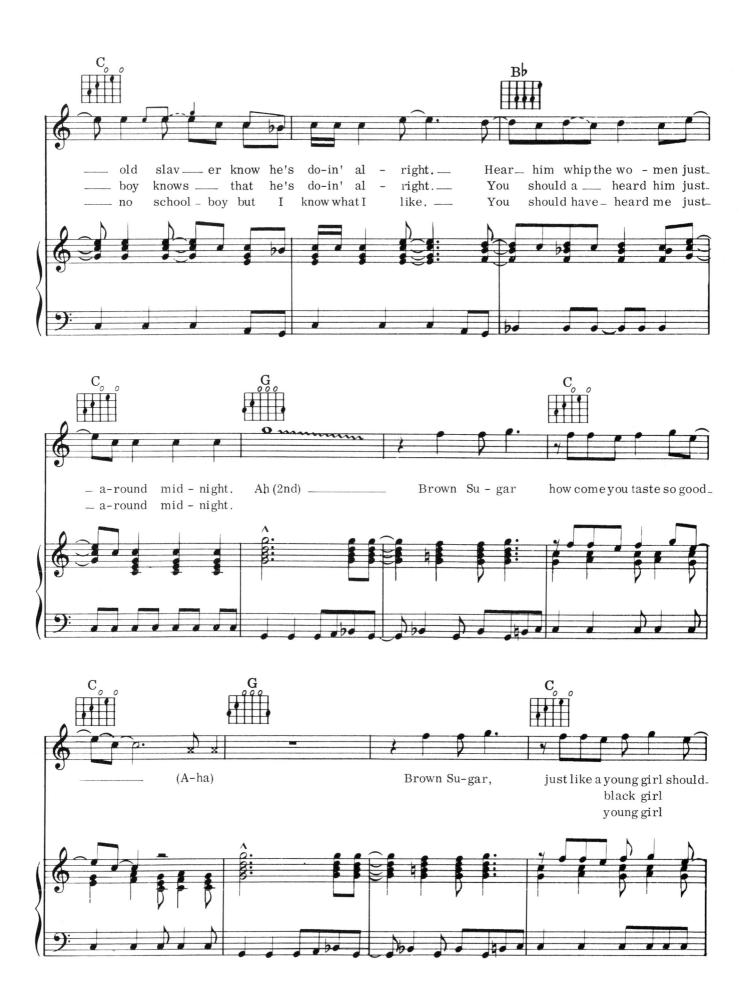

Midnight Rambler

Words & Music: Mick Jagger and Keith Richard

1. Did you hear a-bout the Mid-night Ram-bler?_ Ev-'ry-bod-y got to
2. (Did you hear a-bout the Mid-night Ram-bler?_ He'll leave his foot-prints up and down your

go. Did you hear a-bout the Mid-night Ram-bler,_ The
hall. Did you hear a-bout the Mid-night Ram-bler?_ Did you

one that shut the kitch-en door? He don't give a hoot of warn-
see me make my mid-night call? And if you catch the Mid-night Ram-

ing —   wrapped up   in   a   black cat   cloak. —   He
bler, —   I ll steal your mis-tress from un-der your nose.   Well, go

To Coda ⊕

don't go   in   the light   of   the morn-ing, —   He's split, the time the cock-'rel
eas - y   with your cold fan - dan-go, —   I'll stick my knife right down your

crows.

Talk - in' 'bout the Mid - night Ram-bler, —   the   one you nev - er   seen   be - fore. —

—   Talk - in' 'bout the mid - night   gam - bler, —   Did you

Well, I'm talk-in' 'bout the mid-night gam - bler,___ The

one you've nev - er seen be - fore. _____ Oh, don't do

that. Oh, don't do that. Oh, don't do that.

D.S.al Coda

Did you

Coda

(Spoken)

C9

throat! Ba - by, and it hurts!

Honky Tonk Women

Words & Music: Mick Jagger and Keith Richard

Let's Spend The Night Together

Words & Music: Mick Jagger and Keith Richard

Jumpin' Jack Flash

Words & Music: Mick Jagger and Keith Richard

right   now,   in fact, it's a gas!   But it's all __

right.   I'm Jump-in' Jack Flash, It's a

gas! Gas! Gas! __   I was raised __

I was drowned   I was washed

right thru my head. _____ But it's all

right _____ now, in fact, it's a gas!____

But it's all _____ right, I'm

Jump-in' Jack Flash, It's a gas! Gas! Gas!____

You Can't Always Get What You Want

Words & Music: Mick Jagger and Keith Richard

tion.___ In her glass was a bleed-ing man.___ She was prac-tised at the art ___ of de-

cep - tion; ___ I could tell by her blood - stained hands.___ And You

Chorus:

Can't Al-ways Get What You Want, ___ Hon-ey, ___ You Can't Al-ways Get What You Want. ___ You

Can't Al-ways Get What You Want, _____ But if you try some-time, Yeah, you just might find you get what you need! ___

And You

Ruby Tuesday

Words & Music: Mick Jagger and Keith Richard

The Great Songs of George Harrison.

ISBN 0.7119.0562.2
Order No. AM37649

The Great Songs of Chris DeBurgh.
ISBN 0.7119.0464.2
Order No. AM35536

The Great Songs of Michael Jackson.

ISBN 0.7119.0483.9
Order No. AM36401

The Great Songs of Stevie Wonder.
ISBN 0.7119.0421.9
Order No. AM34596

The Great Songs of The Police.

ISBN 0.7119.0550.9
Order No. AM37565

The Great Songs of Al Stewart.

ISBN 0.7119.0666.1
Order No. AM39587

The Great Songs of John Denver.

ISBN 0.7119.0563.0
Order No. AM37656

The Great Songs of The Carpenters.

ISBN 0.7119.0638.6
Order No. AM39108

The Great Songs of Barry Manilow.

ISBN 0.7119.0561.4
Order No. AM37631

The Great Songs of Cat Stevens.

ISBN 0.7119.0564.9
Order No. AM37664

The Great Songs of The Rolling Stones.

ISBN 0.7119.0593.2
Order No. AM38225

The Great Songs of Rod Stewart.

ISBN 0.7119.0680.7
Order No. AM39694

The Great Songs of Chicago.

ISBN 0.7119.0681.5
Order No. AM39702

The Great Songs of Gordon Lightfoot.

ISBN 0.7119.0391.3
Order No. AM34109

The Great Songs of Chris DeBurgh.

ISBN 0.7119.0697.1
Order No. AM 39900

Great Songs, Great Series.

The greatest songs by the greatest
performers and songwriters of our times.
A handsomely presented, very collectable set of beautifully engraved music,
all in full piano/vocal arrangements with complete lyrics,
guitar chord boxes and symbols.
The most economical way of buying sheet music today.

Available from your local music dealer,
or contact…
Music Sales Limited,
8/9 Frith Street,
London W1V 5TZ.